I Forgive

Written by Catherine A. Haala

Illustrator: Jacqueline Rodriguez
with Blueberry Illustrations

Editor: Bradley Jones

I Forgive: The key to LOVE and PEACE!

Copyright © 2025 Catherine A. Haala

Copyright for all images and illustrations are the sole property of Catherine A. Haala.

All rights reserved. No part of this book may be used or reproduced by any means, graphic, electronic, or mechanical, including photocopying, recording, taping or by any information storage retrieval system without the written permission of the author except in the case of brief quotations embodied in critical articles and reviews.

Haala Publishing
Sleepy Eye, MN

ISBN: 978-1-956726-02-2

Dedicated to the Healing Powers of Forgiveness!

I Forgive

The key to LOVE and PEACE!

Written by Catherine A. Haala

I forgive, I forgive, I forgive I say …

I don't want anything to take my joy away!

If forgiveness doesn't seem fair …

I think of the Law of Attraction …
I am aware!

Do I want more of the same?

Do I really want more and more situations and people to blame?

I close my eyes …
I take a few deep breaths!

I quiet myself …
I go in-depth!

I accept perfect guidance from PERFECT LOVE ...
What is it that serves me?
What do I want more of?

I look for the silver lining …
What hurts no one?
What is wise?

Then the answer does arise …

I choose to be FREEEEEEE!

I forgive others, I forgive me …
We are all a work in process, you and me!

I choose to live in the present …

I choose to live for today …

Nothing can take my power away!

Forgiveness isn't about right or wrong …
Forgiveness is about letting go and moving on!

I refuse to be weighed down by a negative past …

No, no, no …
I choose to be FREEEEEEE at last!

Free to let my light shine brighter than the brightest star, twinkling far and wide …

Touching everyone and everything with peace, love, grace, gratitude, harmony, compassion, joy and pride!

Free to experience the wonder, awe, whimsy and enchantment of everyday miracles …

Free to SMILE the BIGGEST SMILES ever …

Free to shout at the top of my lungs …

"I AM FREEEEEEE!"

"I AM FREEEEEEE!"

"I AM FREEEEEEE!"

I forgive because where there is forgiveness …

There is love …

And where there is love …

There is peace!

I Forgive …

I Love …

www.ingramcontent.com/pod-product-compliance
Lightning Source LLC
Chambersburg PA
CBHW061353010526
44107CB00011B/921